Inventory of Mammals (Excluding Bats) of George Washington Birthplace National Monument

Natural Resource Technical Report NPS/NCBN/NRTR—2010/311

Ronald E. Barry

Bates College
Biology Department
409 Carnegie Science Hall
44 Campus Avenue
Lewiston, Maine 04240

Tressa L. Dolbeare

Department of Biology
201 Compton Science Center
Frostburg State University
101 Braddock Road
Frostburg, Maryland 21532-2303

April 2010

U.S. Department of the Interior
National Park Service
Natural Resource Program Center
Fort Collins, Colorado

The National Park Service, Natural Resource Program Center publishes a range of reports that address natural resource topics of interest and applicability to a broad audience in the National Park Service and others in natural resource management, including scientists, conservation and environmental constituencies, and the public.

The Natural Resource Technical Report Series is used to disseminate results of scientific studies in the physical, biological, and social sciences for both the advancement of science and the achievement of the National Park Service mission. The series provides contributors with a forum for displaying comprehensive data that are often deleted from journals because of page limitations.

All manuscripts in the series receive the appropriate level of peer review to ensure that the information is scientifically credible, technically accurate, appropriately written for the intended audience, and designed and published in a professional manner.

This report received informal peer review by subject-matter experts who were not directly involved in the collection, analysis, or reporting of the data. Data in this report were collected and analyzed using methods based on established, peer-reviewed protocols and were analyzed and interpreted within the guidelines of the protocols.

Views, statements, findings, conclusions, recommendations, and data in this report are those of the author(s) and do not necessarily reflect views and policies of the National Park Service, U.S. Department of the Interior. Mention of trade names or commercial products does not constitute endorsement or recommendation for use by the National Park Service.

This report is available from (http://www.nps.gov/nero/science/) and the Natural Resource Publications Management website (http://www.nature.nps.gov/publications/NRPM).

Please cite this publication as:

Barry, R. E., T. L. Dolbeare. 2010. Inventory of mammals (excluding bats) of George Washington Birthplace Monument. Natural Resource Technical Report NPS/NCBN/NRTR—2010/311. National Park Service, Fort Collins, Colorado.

NPS 332/102045, April 2010

Contents

Figures

Tables

Abstract

A survey of mammals (bats excluded) at George Washington Birthplace National Monument (GEWA) was conducted from 2002 to 2003 to document the presence of ≥ 90% of the mammals in the park, describe their distributions and relative abundances, quantify habitat-specific species diversity, and provide recommendations for management and conservation. Surveys relied on live trapping with Sherman and Tomahawk traps for small to medium-size mammals, the use of pitfall traps to capture small shrews, direct observation of individuals and their sign (tracks, scats), and remote photography. We identified five principal habitats – grassland (fields), mixed deciduous-coniferous forest, pine plantations, logged areas (of mixed forest), and wetlands – and several less expansive habitats, and targeted locations for sampling.

Twenty-one species of mammals were either captured or observed within GEWA, resulting in six new records (species) for the park. Altogether, six orders and 12 families of mammals are represented by these species. Including the new records, we documented 70% (21 of 30) of the species (excluding bats) predicted to occur and 75% (15 of 20) of those for which historical records exist. New species we recorded include the American least shrew (*Cryptotis parva*), southeastern shrew (*Sorex longirostris*), eastern harvest mouse (*Reithrodontomys humulis*), red fox (*Vulpes vulpes*), North American river otter (*Lontra canadensis*), and long-tailed weasel (*Mustela frenata*). The white-footed deermouse (*Peromyscus leucopus*) occupied all of the principal habitats and was the most abundant mammal in the park. Multiple individuals of two grassland specialists, the seldom captured least shrew and spottily distributed eastern harvest mouse, were captured. Also of note, river otters (or their sign) were observed in two locations, on the beach along the Potomac River and along the park's eastern boundary at Popes Creek. Grasslands exhibited the greatest species diversity of small mammals, and logged areas exhibited the least diversity.

The park supports a predictable assemblage of mammals given the diversity of habitats present. Habitat generalists, such as the white-footed deermouse, northern short-tailed shrew (*Blarina brevicauda*), Virginia opossum (*Didelphis virginiana*), raccoon (*Procyon lotor*), and white-tailed deer (*Odocoileus virginianus*), are widely distributed. Adequate quality and quantity of habitat exist to sustain populations of grassland specialists such as the least shrew, eastern harvest mouse, and meadow vole (*Microtus pennsylvanicus*).

Additional inventory and monitoring work should be conducted to determine the status of a number of species either detected in low numbers – the southeastern shrew, marsh oryzomys or rice rat (*Oryzomys palustris*), southern flying squirrel (*Glaucomys volans*), long-tailed weasel – or not confirmed but for which previous records exist – woodland vole (*Microtus pinetorum*), muskrat (*Ondatra zibethicus*), house mouse (*Mus musculus*), brown rat (*Rattus norvegicus*), and mink (*Neovison vison*). This work would necessarily include additional sampling of wetlands and grasslands. A concerted effort should be directed toward documenting the populations of small shrews (*Sorex* spp.) in the park with greater use of pitfall traps (only after proper archeological compliance or oversight has been completed). In addition, the following resource management strategies might be considered, continued, or enhanced: 1) affording special consideration for the protection and conservation of wetlands that support a number of mammal species in GEWA; 2) regulating visitor use of specific areas where sensitive wetland species (e.g, the river otter) are found; 3) maintaining diverse herbaceous communities and interrupting succession in managed fields by careful attention to mowing and burning schedules; 4) acquiring adjoining agricultural land so that it can be managed for native vegetation and mammal species (and reduction in populations of the exotic house mouse); 5) periodically monitoring for exotic house mouse, brown rat, and black rat (*Rattus rattus*) populations; 6) using management practices (e.g., fumigants or live trapping and relocation) to control groundhog (*Marmota monax*) populations; 7) using management practices (e.g., live trapping and relocation) to eliminate problematic mammalian predators such as foxes and weasels that prey on GEWA farm fowl; 8) using management practices that either reduce the raccoon population or the consequences of human activities that sustain it (e.g., more frequent monitoring of picnic areas and trash removal); and 9) monitoring and, if necessary, using management practices to regulate the white-tailed deer population to ensure the preservation of vegetation communities and understory cover important to mammals and birds. Raccoon and white-tailed deer populations, particularly because of rabies and Lyme disease (and abundance of the black-legged [deer] tick larvae and nymph reservoir-competent host, the white-footed deermouse), also are of potential public health significance in a historical park with high human visitation like GEWA.

Acknowledgments

Tressa Dolbeare, M.S. student at FSU and co-author of this report, under the supervision of the senior author conducted the bulk of the field work and prepared voucher specimens for the FSU mammal museum. Rijk Morawe, Chris Upperman, Jeff Schnebelen, and Alan Bateman assisted in the field. We thank Rijk Morawe, Chief of Natural and Cultural Resources Management, for providing information on the park, collection permits, maps, and other materials and for the time he spent introducing us to the park and discussing the project with us. Ralph Eckerlin provided records of voucher specimens housed in the mammal collection at Northern Virginia Community College that were collected in GEWA in the 1980s. John Karish, James Comiskey, Sara Stevens, Bryan Milstead, and Rijk Morawe provided comments on and information for drafts of this report. We are indebted to John Karish, Beth Johnson, Sara Stevens, and the National Park Service for funding the project. Frostburg State University provided much-appreciated matching funds and logistical support.

Introduction

Surveys of mammals in coastal and mid-Atlantic national parks in the Northeast Region are in compliance with the Natural Resource Inventory and Monitoring Program of the National Park Service (NPS 1998). One of the five long-term goals established by this program is to complete baseline inventories of basic biological and geophysical natural resources for the national parks. During Phase 1 of the natural resource inventory the National Park Service (NPS) has set an objective of documenting the presence of ≥ 80% of all plant and animal species (excluding invertebrates) occurring within a park's boundaries; the stated objective for the mammal survey of the parks is 90%. Surveys will attempt to confirm the existence of currently listed species and document the presence of additional expected species. Of particular importance is the detection of any threatened and endangered species that merit special attention. Data collected can be used by park natural resource specialists in the proper stewardship of the park.

We conducted a survey of mammals (except bats, order Chiroptera) in George Washington Birthplace National Monument (GEWA), Virginia, in 2002-2003. The park lies in the Coastal Plain physiographic province east of Fredericksburg, Virginia, in Westmoreland County within the Chesapeake Bay ecosystem (Figure 1). Located on the Northern Neck of rural Virginia, GEWA shares boundaries with tidal portions of the Potomac River, Pope's Creek Estuary, and other historic lands. The monument was authorized by Congress as a unit of the NPS in the Act of January 23, 1930, and opened under the administration of the NPS in 1932. The park's strategic plan (NPS 2004) indicates the need for implementing programs that foster the wise management, restoration and use of natural resources and impeding the invasion, expansion, and establishment of exotic species.

One previous survey of mammals has been conducted in GEWA. That survey produced records for 22 species of mammals, including two species of bats (Painter and Eckerlin 1993). Our inventory work began in summer 2002 and continued through 2003. Surveys included sampling of small to medium-size mammals using Sherman and Tomahawk live traps. Small shrews (*Sorex* spp.) were targeted with arrays of pitfall kill traps so that individuals could be collected for accurate identification to species by skull morphology and dentition. Observations and sign, including scats and road kills, were used to account for mammals squirrel-size and larger.

Figure 1. Location of George Washington Birthplace National Monument (GEWA) in Virginia.

Study Area

The George Washington Birthplace National Monument consists of 223 ha (551 acres) of primarily open grasslands (fields) and upland forests, includes Potomac River beach, and has 10 ha of marshes and estuaries. Its forest resources represent a unique assemblage of loblolly pine and willow oak. Elevation ranges from sea level to nearly 8 m (25 ft.) (Figure 2).

Delineation of habitats

The recognition of major habitat types allowed stratification of the sampling effort in GEWA. This permitted a representative and comprehensive survey of the small mammal fauna by increasing the efficiency with which individual species were detected.

Five principal habitat types – managed fields (grasslands), mixed deciduous-coniferous forest, pine plantations, logged area (within mixed forest), and wetlands (including forested wetlands) – and several less expansive habitats (e.g., deciduous stands, mixed forest/logged area edge, pond edge) were identified for inventorying small mammals in GEWA (Figure 2). In addition, a barn and dormitory lawn were sampled for targeted small mammal species. The secure NPSpecies website, https://science1.nature.nps.gov/npspecies, lists vascular plants certified for the park.

Fields are dominated by broomsedge (*Andropogon virginicus*), Carolina foxtail (*Alopecurus carolinianus*), and other grasses (*Poaceae*), white heath aster (*Aster pilosus*), goldenrod (*Solidago* spp.), and white clover (*Trifolium repens*). Soils are variably loam, clay and sand (including silt loam, clay, clay loam, silty clay, loam, sandy clay loam, fine sandy loam, sand, loamy sand. Fields are brush-hogged once or twice yearly (R. Morawe, pers. comm., George Washington Birthplace National Monument).

Mixed deciduous-coniferous forests constitute approximately 80 ha (200 acres) of the park (Painter and Eckerlin 1993) and are dominated by loblolly pine (*Pinus taeda*), willow oak (*Quercus phellos*), northern red oak (*Quercus rubra*), and swee tgum (*Liquidambar styraciflua*). Soils in mixed forested areas are predominantly loam and clay (including silt loam, silty clay loam, silty clay, clay) (R. Morawe, pers. comm.).

At the beginning of this study the pine plantations were 25-year old stands of loblolly pine, with occasional sweetgum. Soils in the pine plantations are predominantly loam and clay (including silt loam, clay loam, silty clay loam, silty clay, clay) (R. Morawe, pers. comm.)

The approximately 5-ha (12-acre) logged area was cut within the mixed forest in 1995. Loblolly pine is now the most abundant tree in the logged area, with significant numbers of red maple (*Acer rubrum*) and sweetgum. Deciduous stands near the logged area and within one of the pine plantations are dominated by sweetgum, with loblolly pine and eastern red cedar (Juniperus virginiana) present.

Wetlands are dominated by common greenbriar (*Smilax rotundifolia*), American holly (*Ilex opaca*), wax myrtle (*Myrica cerifera*), and willow oak. Additional species found in wetlands include narrowleaf cattail (*Typha angustifolia*), smartweed (*Polygonum* spp.), poison-ivy (*Toxicodendron radicans*), eastern baccharis (*Baccharis halimifolia*), white oak (*Quercus alba*), pin oak (*Quercus. palustris*), red oak, black gum (*Nyssa sylvatica*), sweetgum, and loblolly pine.

Soils are sand and clay (R Morawe, pers. comm.., Georgre Washington Birthplace National Monument). Dominant vegetation associated with the forest/swamp edge includes greenbriar, willow oak, sweetgum, American holly, and red oak. Woody vegetation in pond-edge habitat consists of hackberry (*Celtis occidentalis*), paw paw (*Asimina triloba*), and sweetgum. Soils are loam and clay (including silty clay loam, silty clay, clay, sandy clay, loam, sandy clay loam, clay loam) (R. Morawe, pers. comm.).

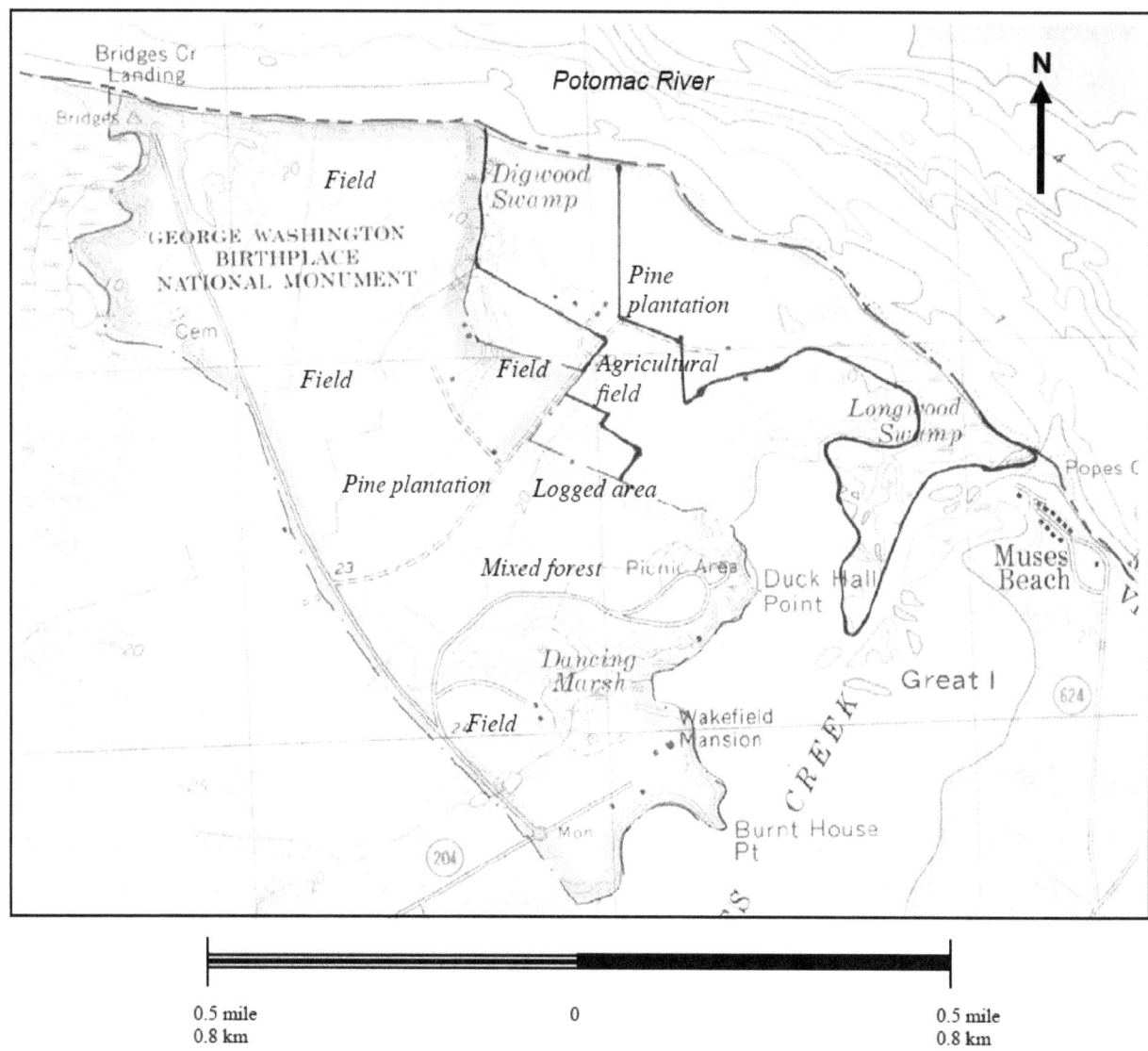

Figure 2. Map showing features and habitat types of George Washington Birthplace National Monument (the most inclusive area outlined).

Methods

Sampling protocol

Sampling sites were located within the five identified habitat types to permit stratified sampling. In addition, unusual or less common habitats (e.g., barn and dormitory lawn) were sampled opportunistically because they often harbor small populations or rare or exotic species. Habitats initially were identified by aerial photo (Figure 3). Strata were ground-truthed before final selection of sampling sites. The number of sampling locations (sample units) was dependent on 1) number, size and distribution of habitat types, and 2) constraints imposed by accessibility, equipment, and personnel.

To identify sampling points a systematic grid (composed of 30 x 30-m cells) of UTM coordinates was overlaid on an aerial photograph that depicted habitat types (NPS 2000; Figure 3). Points on the grid, within a habitat type, were selected without replacement by the generation of random numbers representing grid cells (Rudran and Foster 1996). Once selected on a map, a sampling point was identified in real space using a Garmin 12 or comparable GPS unit. Portions of the park frequented by the public, and areas inaccessible to ground personnel, generally were removed from consideration as sampling locations after the initial visit.

Sampling of small mammals relied primarily on capture with rat-sized (7.6 x 8.9 x 22.9 cm) Sherman live traps. These traps are generally highly effective for capture of rodents and large shrews such as *Blarina* spp. (Mitchell et al. 1993). Pitfall traps were used to capture shrews and small mammals < 10 g (Kirkland and Sheppard 1994). Pitfalls for shrews were used as kill-type traps containing 3-5 cm of water because careful measurements and examination of skull morphology, dentition, and internal anatomy were required for identification of species, sex, and reproductive condition (Caldwell and Bryan 1982).

Sherman traps were configured at sampling points in randomly positioned linear transects and grids (Table 1; Appendices A and C), with a trap interval of 10 or 15 m. Trap configuration and number of traps (i.e., grid size or transect length) was dependent on habitat type, patch size, availability of traps, and need for detailed demographic information. Transects were used where practical because they traverse more home ranges per effort than grids and are especially appropriate for inventory work where accurate estimates of abundance or density are not necessary (Jones et al. 1996). Effective sampling area of a grid was computed by adding a boundary strip equal to one-half the trap interval to all four sides of the grid (Krebs 1999). Effective sampling length of a transect was computed by adding one-half trap interval to each end of the transect. Sampling periods of consecutive days of trapping ranged from 1 to 8 days. This sampling regime permitted estimates of species richness and relative abundance (unique individuals per 100 trap nights) for the principal habitat types. While sampling for small mammals at designated locations, we also observed and noted sign of larger mammals; species, location, and date for each such observation were recorded.

Figure 3. USGS aerial photograph of George Washington Birthplace National Monument (within green line) showing points sampled in 2002 and 2003. AG = agricultural, DF = deciduous stand, FLD = field, LOG = logged area, MF = mixed deciduous-coniferous forest, MF/LOG = mixed forest/logged area edge, PP = pine plantation, Pond = pond edge, WL = wetland, PT indicates proximity to the Potomac River. Black indicates agricultural field adjacent to the park that was sampled in 2003.

Table 1. Sherman trap configuration for sampling sites at George Washington Birthplace National Monument for 2002 and 2003.

Year	Habitat/Site[1]	Sherman Trap Configuration[2]	Trap Nights			
			Sherman Traps	Tomahawk Traps[3]	Pitfall Array	Mole Harpoon Traps
2002						
	FLD 1	Transect (0.30)	120	8^m		
	FLD 2	Grid (0.49)	196	16^m		
	FLD 3	Transect (0.24)	48			
	MF 1	Grid (0.49)	196	16^m		
	MF 2	Grid (0.49)	196	16^m		
	DF	Grid (0.49)	98			
	PP 1	Grid (0.49)	196	16^m		
	WL 2	Transect (0.09)	36			
2003						
	FLD 1	Transect (0.14)	322			
	PT FLD 1	Transect (0.45)	120			
	PT FLD 2	Transect (0.45)	120			
	MF	Grid (1.10)	3049	59^m	18	
	MF 1				66	
	MF/LOG	Transect (0.30)	520	$3^s, 10^m$		
	DF in PP 1	Transect (0.15)	30			
	PP 1	Grid (1.10)	3105	51^m		
	PP 2	Grid (1.10)	196		63	
	LOG 1	Grid (1.12)	2850	59^m		
	LOG 2	Grid (0.32)	322	9^s		
	WL 3	Transect (0.08)	20	$9^s, 3^m$		
	WL 4	Transect (0.45)	120	12^s		
	Digwood Swamp	Transect (0.32)	84	$16^s, 8^m$		
	PT Pond			$8^s, 4^m$		
	Barn	Random	21			
	Dorm Lawn					32

[1] DF = deciduous forest, FLD = field, LOG = logged area, MF = mixed deciduous-coniferous forest, MF/LOG = mixed forest/logged area edge, Pond = pond edge, PP = pine plantation, WL = wetland. PT = near the Potomac River. See Figure 3 for site locations within GEWA.
[2] Numbers in parentheses for Sherman trap configuration represent effective sampling areas in ha for grids and effective sampling lengths in km for transects.
[3] Tomahawk live traps (^{s} = small, ^{m} = medium)

Muskrat- (small – 15.2 x 15.2 x 48.3 cm) and raccoon-size (medium - 25.4 x 30.5 x 81.3 cm) Tomahawk live traps were used to capture mammals of squirrel size and larger, butparticularly to target mesocarnivores such as raccoons (*Procyon lotor*) and red (*Vulpes vulpes*) and gray (*Urocyon cinereoargenteus*) foxes. One to several of these traps were placed in small mammal (Sherman) trapping grids and transects (Appendix D) and opportunistically in habitats where mammal sign was detected or where habitat features suggested the presence of larger species. Pitfall traps were arranged in arrays. Each array was 10 m long and consisted of a silt fence and pitfall trap (#10 vegetable can) at each end and in the middle. Each array was placed in association within a Sherman trap grid and at least 30 m from another array. Remote cameras were used sporadically to document the presence of larger, secretive and elusive species (such as foxes) where sign was evident.

Dominant vegetation, percent canopy cover, percent ground cover, degree of disturbance (e.g., primary or secondary forest or plantation, agricultural use of grassland), soil type, presence of rock piles, topography and elevation were noted for each sampling site at 5-15 (proportional to the number of Sherman traps) random locations within Sherman live-trap transects and grids (McDiarmid and Wilson 1996; Barry et al. 1999; Boyce 2001). These detailed observations were recorded as baseline habitat information.

Sherman traps were baited with a combination of peanut butter and rolled oats. Tomahawk traps usually were baited with canned cat food. Pitfall, mole harpoon traps, and remote camera locations were not baited. Captured individuals of small species (those in Sherman and pitfall traps) were removed from traps, identified to species, weighed using a Pesola scale, and examined for age, sex, and reproductive condition (Jones et al. 1996). Individuals captured in Tomahawk traps were identified to species and examined for age, sex, and reproductive condition. Because recognition of individuals was used for determining relative abundances and measures of species diversity, captured individuals of small mammal species were marked by toe-clipping (Rudran 1996; ASM 1998). To obtain meaningful scientific data about shrews, they were collected by kill trapping (see above). Release of captured individuals (other than shrews or accidental deaths) was immediate at the capture location after measurements were obtained. Live-trapping, handling procedures, pitfall trapping, and specimen collection were conducted humanely (Rudran and Kunz 1996), consistent with the animal handling guidelines of the American Society of Mammalogists (ASM 1998), and were approved by the Institutional Review Board/Animal Care and Use Committee (IACUC # A2002-01) at Frostburg State University. Proper precautions were taken by investigators to prevent human injury and exposure to disease, especially rabies, Lyme disease, hantaviral pulmonary syndrome (HPS), and human ehrlichiosis (Gage et al. 1995; Mills et al. 1995; Kunz et al. 1996). Animals found dead in traps (most frequently in pitfalls), if salvageable, were collected, prepared, deposited, and maintained in the Frostburg State University (FSU) mammal museum.

Yearly Sampling Protocol
Sampling using Sherman and medium Tomahawk live traps was conducted in five habitats – managed fields (grassland), pine plantation, mixed deciduous-coniferous forest, a small tract of deciduous forest, and wetland – in nine sampling periods from July through November 2002 (Table 1; see Appendix A). At nine sampling points Sherman traps comprised six grids (7 x 7 traps each) covering a total of 2.9 ha (7.2 acres) and three transects of variable length along 0.6 km (0.4 miles). Sherman trap interval was 10 m for all transects and grids. Trap nights totaled

1,282 trap nights with Sherman traps and 88 with Tomahawk traps. In addition to these sampling periods, direct observations of mammals (or their sign) and remote photography yielded records of mammals in May and July.

Sherman, small and medium Tomahawk live traps, and pitfall traps were opened during 31 sampling periods (typically three to four nights each) from March through December 2003. We sampled managed field (grassland), mixed deciduous-coniferous forest, pine plantation, logged area, wetland, pond edge (PT Pond), and mixed forest/logged area edge (MF/LOG) habitat, a barn, and a lawn (Table 1; Appendixes C, D). At 13 sampling locations where Sherman traps were used, five grids (3 x 10, 5 x 10, or 7 x 7 traps, depending on size and shape of the patch) covered a total of 4.7 ha (11.6 acres), and eight transects of variable length spanned a total of 2.3 km (1.4 miles). Sherman traps were placed randomly at the barn location in an attempt to capture house mice and rats. Traps were spaced at 15-m intervals in grids and transects, except for FLD 1 where we used 10-m intervals (i.e., a higher concentration of traps per linear space; Appendix C) in a location where we failed to capture any mammals in 2002. Twenty-one pitfalls (7 arrays) total were used at three locations (Appendix D). Six locations were sampled with small Tomahawk traps, and seven were sampled with medium Tomahawk traps (Appendix D). Pitfall arrays and Tomahawk traps were spatially associated with Sherman traps. Four mole (harpoon) kill traps were used in the dormitory lawn (Appendix D) to obtain a voucher specimen of the eastern mole (*Scalopus aquaticus*). Trap nights totaled 10,849 with Sherman traps, 57 with small Tomahawk traps, 194 with medium Tomahawk traps, 147 with pitfall arrays, and 32 with harpoon traps in 2003. Higher numbers of trap nights with traps in grid configurations in mixed forest, pine plantation, and logged habitat are attributable to targeted sampling for a study of the comparative demography of *Peromyscus leucopus* in these three habitat types (Dolbeare, in prep.).

Compilation and analysis of data

Species distributions among habitats were summarized. Marking and recognition of individuals captured in Sherman traps permitted estimates of relative abundance, species diversity (Brillouin's *H*), rarefaction estimates of richness (number of species), and Smith and Wilson's measure of evenness (distribution of individuals among the species) for small species for principal habitat types. Analyses followed Krebs (1999) and were conducted at Frostburg State University using EcoMeth software (Krebs 2003).

Data on habitat characteristics and all mammals captured or observed were stored in an electronic database (Microsoft Access). Voucher specimens were prepared and accessioned into the mammal museum at Frostburg State University. Color photographs taken with digital and remote cameras were stored and copies provided to the Chief of Natural and Cultural Resources Management of the park.

Results

Historical records and predicted species

The National Park Service's NPSpecies database (https://science1.nature.nps.gov/npspecies) contains historical records of plants and animals for each park. Publications and park records pertaining to the mammals of GEWA were sought, and the summary of existing records was obtained from the NPSpecies database. The 20 species of mammals (bats excluded) recorded in the NPSpecies database resulted from a survey conducted by Painter and Eckerlin (1993), who deposited a number of specimens as vouchers in the collection at Northern Virginia Community College in Annandale, Virginia (Appendix F). According to current taxonomy (Wilson and Reeder 2005), six orders and 12 families are represented among the species recorded prior to this report (Table 2).

We have listed species predicted to occur in GEWA (Table 2) based on Virginia GAP species range maps, Webster et al. (1985), and Linzey (1998). This list contains 30 species within six orders and 14 families of mammals (excluding bats).

Field survey

Our survey of 2002-2003 resulted in 21 species of mammals either captured or observed within GEWA. These results included six new species records for the park (Table 2). The species detected belong to six orders and 12 families of mammals.

In 2002 30 individuals representing five species of mammals were captured a total of 54 times at six of the nine sampling locations and a targeted location, a horse pasture (Appendixes A and B). In 2003 216 individuals representing 14 species of mammals were captured a total of 530 times at 16 of the 17 sampling locations (Appendixes C, D, and E). Types of habitats, sampling dates, numbers of trap nights, individuals captured, capture frequencies, and relative abundances for mammal species are summarized for each sampling location, by year, in Appendixes A-E.

The most abundant small mammal in GEWA was the white-footed deermouse, *Peromyscus leucopus*. This species was captured in Sherman traps in all five principal habitats and mixed forest/logged area edge (Table 3) and was the most abundant species in mixed forest, pine plantation, logged areas, wetland, and mixed forest/logged area edge. The northern short-tailed shrew was captured in Sherman traps in all habitat types except the logged area, although in relatively low numbers. The white-footed deermouse also was captured more often with pitfall traps than any other species. These traps, used sparingly in 2003 in mixed forest (MF and MF 1; see Appendix D) and pine plantation 2, were successful only in the pine plantation where four white-footed deermice (relative abundance = 6.35), three northern short-tailed shrews (*Blarina brevicauda*; relative abundance = 4.76), and a southeastern shrew (*Sorex longirostris*; relative abundance = 1.59) were captured.

Table 2. Comparison of predicted species for GEWA (based on Gap Analysis, http://gapmap.nbii.gov/generatemap.php?species=GENUS%SPECIES&statelist=VA, Webster et al. 1985, and Linzey 1998), historical records (Painter and Eckerlin 1993), and species observed during this study (2002-2003). Taxonomy and common names follow Wilson and Reeder (2005).

Order Family	Species	Common Name	Predicted	GEWA Historical	GEWA Observed
Didelphimorphia					
Didelphidae	*Didelphis virginiana*	Virginia opossum	X	X	X
Soricomorpha					
Soricidae	*Blarina brevicauda*	Northern short-tailed shrew	X	X	X
	Cryptotis parva	North American least shrew	X		X
	Sorex hoyi	American pygmy shrew	X		
	Sorex longirostris	Southeastern shrew	X		X
Talpidae	*Condylura cristata*	Star-nosed mole	X		
	Scalopus aquaticus	Eastern mole	X	X	X
Lagomorpha					
Leporidae	*Sylvilagus floridanus*	Eastern cottontail	X	X	X
Rodentia					
Castoridae	*Castor canadensis*	American beaver	X·	X	X
Cricetidae	*Microtus pennsylvanicus*	Meadow vole	X	X	X
	Microtus pinetorum	Woodland vole	X	X	
	Ondatra zibethicus	Common muskrat	X	X	
	Oryzomys palustris	Marsh oryzomys (rice rat)	X	X	X
	Peromyscus leucopus	White-footed deermouse	X	X	X
	Reithrodontomys humulis	Eastern harvest mouse	X		X
Muridae	*Mus musculus*	House mouse	X	X	
	Rattus norvegicus	Brown rat	X	X	
Sciuridae	*Glaucomys volans*	Southern flying squirrel	X	X	X
	Marmota monax	Woodchuck	X	X	X
	Sciurus carolinensis	Eastern gray squirrel	X	X	X
	Tamias striatus	Eastern chipmunk	X		
Carnivora					
Canidae	*Urocyon cinereoargenteus*	Gray fox	X	X	X
	Vulpes vulpes	Red fox	X		X
Felidae	*Lynx rufus*	Bobcat	X		
Mephitidae	*Mephitis mephitis*	Striped skunk	X	X	X
Mustelidae	*Lontra Canadensis*	North American river otter	X		X
	Mustela frenata	Long-tailed weasel	X		X
	Neovison vison	American mink	X	X	
Procyonidae	*Procyon lotor*	Raccoon	X	X	X
Artiodactyla					
Cervidae	*Odocoileus virginianus*	White-tailed deer	X	X	X

Table 3. Summary of numbers and relative abundances[1] of small mammals captured with Sherman traps among five principal habitat types[2] and one edge habitat at George Washington Birthplace National Park, 2002-2003.

Common name	Species name	Habitat					
		FLD	MF	PP	LOG	WL	MF/LOG
Northern short-tailed shrew	*Blarina brevicauda*	2(0.20)	5(0.15)	1(0.03)		1(0.26)	1(0.19)
American least shrew	*Cryptotis parva*	7(0.70)					
Meadow vole	*Microtus pennsylvanicus*	10(1.00)					
Marsh oryzomys	*Oryzomys palustris*						2(0.53)
White-footed deermouse	*Peromyscus leucopus*	4(0.40)	37(1.08)	44(1.26)	64(2.02)	20(5.26)	15(2.88)
Eastern harvest mouse	*Reithrodontomys humulis*	2(0.20)			1(0.03)		
Southern flying squirrel	*Glaucomys volans*			1(0.03)			
Long-tailed weasel	*Mustela frenata*				1(0.03)		
Total number of trap nights		1,002	3,441	3,595	3,172	380	520

[1] Relative abundance calculated as the number of individuals per 100 trap nights and shown in parentheses
[2] FLD = fields, MF = mixed deciduous-coniferous forest, PP = pine plantations, LOG = logged area, WL = wetland, MF/LOG = mixed forest/logged area edge.

Several species were associated solely or primarily with field habitats. The meadow vole (*Microtus pennsylvanicus*) was the most abundant species found in field habitat (Table 3). American least shrews (*Cryptotis parva*) were abundant in one field (FLD 1; Appendix E) in 2003. The eastern harvest mouse (*Reithrodontomys humulis*) was found in two fields and logged area 1, and two individuals of this species were captured in only 21 Sherman trap nights in thebarn (relative abundance = 9.52). An eastern mole (*Scalopus aquaticus*) was captured in a harpoon trap in the dormitory lawn area.

Several other species were captured infrequently in Sherman traps. Two marsh rice rats (*Oryzomys palustris*) were captured in Dancing Marsh (WL 3; Appendix E) at the southern end of the park. One southern flying squirrel (*Glaucomys volans*) was caught in pine plantation 1. A single long-tailed weasel was captured in logged area 1.

Capture frequencies of larger mammals captured in Tomahawk traps were recorded, but relative abundances were not obtained because individuals of these larger species were not marked for individual recognition. No captures occurred in 2002. In 2003 Virginia opossums (*Didelphis virginiana*) and raccoons (*Procyon lotor*) were distributed widely within the park, occurring in all four of the principal habitats sampled (Table 4). In addition, raccoons were captured in the mixed forest/logged area and pond edge habitats (see Appendix E). Striped skunks (*Mephitis mephitis*) were documented in the mixed forest. We captured a female opossum with a juvenile while we were targeting foxes near a den in the horse pasture about 5 m from the edge of woods.

Thirteen species of mammals were documented based on either observation or sign during the study. Four of these species – the white-footed deermouse, striped skunk (*Mephitis mephitis*), raccoon, and white-tailed deer (*Odocoileus virginianus*) - were documented by remote camera (Table 5). A white-footed deermouse was photographed in the mouth of a Barred Owl (*Strix varia*) in November 2002. Raccoons were photographed on two occasions in pine plantation 1. White- tailed deer (*Odocoileus virginianus*) were observed frequently, most often in fields near forest, and photographed in pine plantation 1. A striped skunk was photographed in a deciduous stand in pine plantation 1.

Mole sign was observed in historical areas and the dormitory lawn in the southern portion of the park. Eastern cottontails (*Sylvilagus floridanus*) were observed often in open, grassy areas, and in pond-edge and wetland habitat (Longwood Swamp) near the Potomac River. A beaver (*Castor canadensis*) lodge was found in Digwood Swamp, and an individual was observed swimming in the pond near the dormitory. Eastern gray squirrels (*Sciurus carolinensis*) were observed frequently in open areas within the park or on roads adjacent to wooded habitat, and woodchucks (*Marmota monax*) were seen and documented most often in grassy areas and along roads.

Of particular note, multiple tracks of North American river otters (*Lontra canadensis*) were observed on the beach at 1324 h on 24 July 2002, and three otters were seen along Popes Creek at 1400 h on 24 August 2003. We saw a gray fox (*Urocyon cinereogenteus*) in a field near the Potomac River at 1030 h on 24 March 2003 and a red fox (*Vulpes vulpes*) in a field near the maintenance area at 1000 h on 24 September 2003. Domestic dogs (*Canis familiaris*) were observed roaming in the park on a few occasions but were assumed to be from nearby residences and not included in the inventory.

Table 4. Total captures of mammals in Tomahawk traps1 among four principal habitat types and one edge habitat at George Washington Birthplace National Park, 2002-2003.

Common name	Species name	Habitat				
		MF	PP	LOG	WL	MF/LOG
Virginia opossum	*Didelphis virginiana*	3	3	2	1	
Raccoon	*Procyon lotor*	4	2	9	2	3
Striped skunk	*Mephitis mephitis*	2				

[1] See Appendices 1 and 3 for trap nights for each size Tomahawk trap in each habitat.
[2] MF = mixed deciduous-coniferous forest, PP = pine plantations, LOG = logged area, WL = wetland, MF/LOG = mixed forest/logged area edge.

Table 5. Mammal sightings or sign in George Washington Birthplace National Monument, 2002-2003.

Common name	Scientific Name	Means of Observation		
		Direct Observation	Signs or Remains	Remote Camera
Eastern mole	Scalopus aquaticus	X	X	
White-footed deermouse	Peromyscus leucopus			X
Eastern cottontail	Sylvilagus floridanus	X		
American beaver	Castor canadensis	X	X	
Eastern gray squirrel	Sciurus carolinensis	X	X	
Woodchuck	Marmota monax	X		
Domestic dog	Canis lupus	X [a]		
Gray fox	Urocyon cinereoargenteus	X	X	
Red fox	*Vulpes vulpes*	X		
Striped skunk	Mephitis mephitis	X		X
North American river otter	Lontra canadensis	X	X	
Raccoon	Procyon lotor	X		X
White-tailed deer	Odocoileus virginianus	X	X	X

[a] Not included in the inventory

Species diversity and evenness of small mammals captured with Sherman traps was greatest in grassy fields and lowest in the logged area (Table 6). Similarly, species richness was greatest in grassy fields where five species were captured (Table 3) in a total of 1,002 trap nights; only three species were caught in the logged area in 3,172 trap nights. At a sample size of 15 individuals asa basis for comparison of richness among habitats, the rarefaction estimate of expected number of species for fields was nearly twice that for wetlands, the habitat with the next highest estimated richness (Figure 4).

Voucher specimens

Thirty-one specimens of eight species were collected from GEWA and prepared, assigned NPS accession and catalog numbers, and accessioned into the FSU mammal museum in 2004 (Table 7). Seventeen of the preparations consisted of skin and skull. Multiple preparations were made of northern short-tailed shrews, least shrews, and white-footed deermice. In addition, three specimens of house mice, *Mus musculus*, were collected from the agricultural field we sampled just outside the park (Figure 3); these specimens were prepared as museum skins and skull and accessioned into the FSU mammal museum.

Table 6. Brillouin diversity index (*H*, determined using $\log_2$) and Smith and Wilson's measure of evenness (Krebs 1999) for small mammals captured in five habitats and one edge habitat in George Washington Birthplace National Monument, 2002-2003.

Habitat	Brillouin Index (*H*)	Smith and Wilson's Evenness
Fields	1.720	0.746
Mixed forest	0.469	0.500
Pine plantations	0.239	0.194
Logged areas	0.183	0.162
Wetlands	0.538	0.349
Mixed forest/logged area edge	0.250	0.318

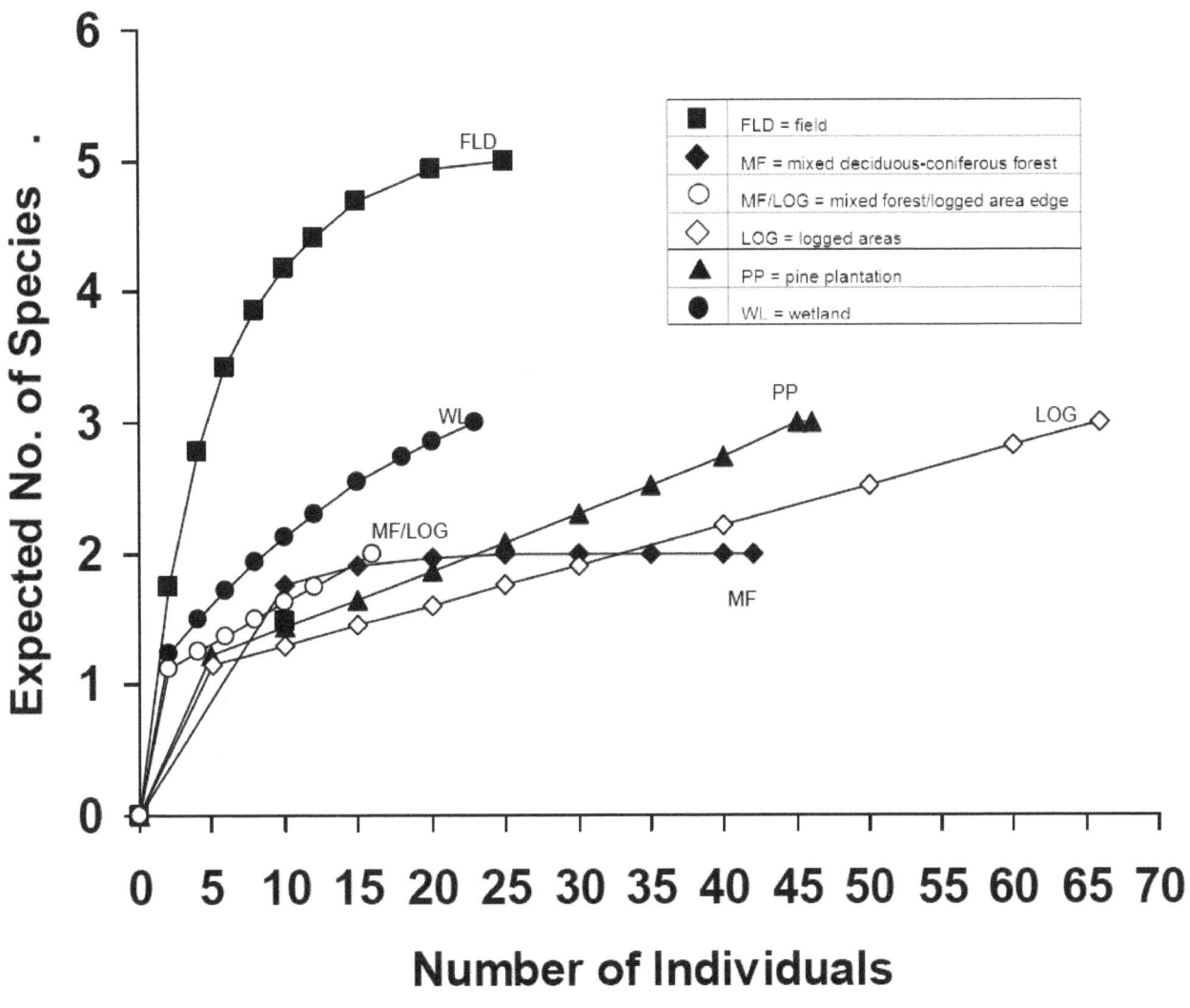

Figure 4. Rarefaction curves showing the estimated number of species of small mammals for variable sample sizes (number of individuals) for six habitat types in George Washington Birthplace National Monument.

Table 7. Specimens collected in George Washington Birthplace National Monument that were assigned NPS accession and catalog numbers and accessioned into the FSU mammal collection (museum) in 2004.

Common Name	Scientific Name	Sex	Specimen Type[1]	NPS Accession/ Catalog Numbers	FSU Catalog Number
Northern short-tailed shrew	*Blarina brevicauda*	F	Sk	1770/21002	2661
		F	SS	1770/21002	2662
		M	SS	1770/21002	2663
		F	SS	1770/21002	2668
		M	Sl	1770/21002	2675
		F	Sl	1770/21002	2677
			Sl	1770/21002	2679
		F	Sl	1770/21002	2680
		M	Sk	1770/21002	2682
American least shrew	*Cryptotis parva*		SS	1770/21009	2656
		F	SS	1770/21009	2658
		F	SS	1770/21009	2660
		F	Sl	1770/21009	2670
		F	Sl	1770/21009	2672
Southeastern shrew	*Sorex longirostris*	F	Sl	1770/21005	2657
Eastern mole	*Scalopus aquaticus*	M	SS	1770/21008	2665
White-footed deermouse	*Peromyscus leucopus*	F	SS	1770/21001	2646
		M	SS	1770/21001	2647
		F	SS	1770/21001	2648
		M	SS	1770/21001	2649
		M	SS	1770/21001	2650
		M	SS	1770/21001	2651
		M	SS	1770/21001	2652
		F	SS	1770/21001	2653
		M	SS	1770/21001	2654
		F	Sl	1770/21001	2673
		M	Sl	1770/21001	2676
			Sl	1770/21001	2678
Southern flying squirrel	*Glaucomys volans*	F	SS	1770/21007	2666
Eastern gray squirrel	*Sciurus carolinensis*	M	SS	1770/21006	2667
Gray fox	*Urocyon cinereoargenteus*		Sl	1770/21003	2681

[1] Sk = skin, Sl = skull, SS = skin and skull.

Discussion

Species records

Including the six new records, we have documented the presence in GEWA of 70% (21 of 30) of the species predicted to occur and 75% (15 of 20) of the nonchiropteran species listed for GEWA on NPSpecies. We were not able to confirm by capture or observation the presence of the following species for which there are historical records: woodland vole (*Microtus pinetorum*), muskrat (*Ondatra zibethicus*), house mouse, brown rat, and mink (*Neovison vison*). The recent switch by GEWA personnel to new storage bins for livestock food apparently has reduced or eliminated rats in the food storage area.

Habitat generalists

The white-footed deermouse is a woodland species that is present statewide (Linzey 1998). It was captured more frequently than any other species in Sherman traps in all of the principal habitat types except fields and is the most frequently captured mammal in park structures (R. Morawe, pers. comm.). It commonly occupies brushy habitat or wooded areas dominated by deciduous species and ample, downed woody debris (Barry and Francq 1980; Lackey et al. 1985). Its predominance in the logged area in GEWA is consistent with the results of other studies that have demonstrated its abundance in recently logged sites. For instance, Buckner and Shure (1985) found that this species in the southern Appalachians reached high densities in forest openings created by clearcuts with ample stumps, logs, and other low-lying cover. Kirkland (1990) observed high numbers of captures in sapling-pole stands (8-18 years post-clearcutting).

The northern short-tailed shrew occurs within a wide variety of habitats throughout its range(George et al. 1986) and was distributed widely in GEWA. We captured this species in all habitats except the logged area, although one individual was captured within the mixed forest/logged area edge. Numbers were not high at any of the sampling locations, but relative abundance was high in pine plantation 2. Absence in the logged area may be due to reduced canopy cover and a poorly developed leaf litter layer, contributing to a dry substrate. Merritt (1987) suggested that short-tailed shrews may avoid dry areas. Mammone (1997) found this species associated with herbaceous ground cover and leaf litter but not logs in clearcuts and adjacent woodlands in western Maryland.

The southeastern shrew is a diminutive species that is captured more commonly with pitfall traps. Our detection of this species in GEWA represents a new record for the park. We captured only one, in a pitfall trap in the pine plantation. Nevertheless, it has been found in a variety of habitats within its range, although it seems to be more abundant in wet areas bordering marshes, swamps or rivers (French 1980). In this case, GEWA would seem to present abundant habitat for this species. We likely would have captured more individuals if we had used pitfall traps around wetlands and in wet areas along or near the river.

Eastern cottontails, gray squirrels, and woodchucks were observed frequently in open, grassy areas, cultivated fields, field-forest edges, and urban parks; we documented all three species in open areas within GEWA. Eastern cottontails are widely distributed among habitats within their range (Chapman et al. 1980), although they prefer old fields, brushy areas, field-woodland edge (Linzey 1998), and early successional habitat (Chapman and Litvaitis 2003). Eastern gray squirrels are most common in mature, intact deciduous and mixed deciduous-coniferous woodlands but use a variety of habitats throughout their range (Koprowski 1994; Linzey 1998; Edwards et al. 2003). Woodchucks typically occupy field-forest ecotone (Kwiecinski 1998). GEWA provides numerous grassy patches adjacent to forest tracts capable of supporting healthy populations of these three species.

The raccoon and Virginia opossum exhibit a wide breadth of habitat use, with predilection for wooded areas near water (McManus 1974; Lotze and Anderson 1979; Gardner and Sunquist 2003; Gehrt 2003). Both species were distributed widely within the park and were captured within all four of the principal habitat types sampled with Tomahawk traps, including wetlands. The raccoon was persistent in the logged area and also was captured in the mixed forest/logged area edge. In addition, it was photographed within pine plantation habitat by remote camera. Wetland habitat within GEWA, including Digwood and Longwood swamps, Dancing Marsh, Potomac River beach and associated riparian habitat, several small ponds, wetland at the northwestern boundary, and intervening mixed forest provide ideal habitat for the opossum and raccoon.

The detection of striped skunks only in mixed forest and a deciduous stand in the pine plantation was somewhat surprising, given that it is a habitat generalist. We suspect that skunks in GEWA visit a variety of habitats as they move from place to place within their home ranges to forage primarily on insects, notably beetles (Rosatte and Lariviere 2003).

Our detection of the long-tailed weasel in GEWA represents a new record for the park. Although this mammal is a habitat generalist, it is generally found close to standing water (Sheffield and Thomas 1997). We captured only one individual in GEWA, probably because this species is at the upper size limit for capture in rat-sized Sherman traps and is too small to be contained within medium and large Tomahawk traps. We suspect this species is widespread within the park because of ample suitable habitat and small mammal prey.

A single gray fox was observed in a field in both our study and in that conducted by Painter and Eckerlin (1993). Both gray and red foxes traverse a variety of habitats within their considerable home ranges. Gray foxes are more often associated with woodlands and red foxes with fragmented landscapes, but gray foxes in eastern North America prefer a mix of fields and forest (Cypher 2003). The resource requirements of both species are provided by the diversity of habitat and small mammal fauna found in GEWA and the surrounding terrain. Our observation of a red fox represents a new species record for GEWA.

White-tailed deer are cosmopolitan in their habitat affinities, occupying both open and forested habitats (Miller et al. 2003). Nevertheless, they are most often associated with woodlands (Linzey 1998). We observed them often in fields near forest (where they are most visible), but they also were seen and photographed remotely in forested habitats. They appear to be abundant in GEWA with its diversity of habitats that provide concealment and thermal cover and satisfy the foraging needs of this species.

Habitat specialists
The most abundant small mammal in GEWA fields was the meadow vole. This mammal is found primarily in open grasslands (Reich 1981; Linzey 1998). The least shrew also was common in GEWA fields. Our discovery of this species represents a new record for GEWA.

Typical habitat for the least shrew is grassy fields (Whitaker 1974; Linzey 1998). The eastern harvest mouse was captured in two fields, a logged area (LOG 1) and the barn. In addition, several were captured in 2003 in the agricultural field adjoining the park. Detection of this species in GEWA represents a new record for the park. This species has been found primarily in old fields (Stalling 1997) containing plants such as broomsedge (*Andropogon* spp.) and goldenrod (*Solidago* spp.), two prominent taxa in GEWA fields.

The marsh rice rat is semiaquatic and found most often in wetland habitats (Wolfe 1982). The rice rat is an important species at GEWA where it is approaching the northern extreme of its geographic range. Painter and Eckerlin (1993) trapped them frequently in marshes and wet meadows in the 1980s in GEWA. We suspect that more intensive sampling of the abundant wetland habitats in the park would demonstrate a still healthy population of marsh rice rats.

We captured and observed sign of eastern moles in the soft soil of the dormitory lawn and historical areas of the park. Soil type is a limiting factor for the eastern mole, which prefers moist soils of loam or sand and avoids clay and gravel (Yates and Schmidly 1978). Within this restriction this species can be found in meadows, gardens, cultivated fields, forests, and river bottoms (Linzey 1998). Painter and Eckerlin (1993) captured one individual in 1988 and found runways (tunnels) in the sandy soil near Pope's Creek.

Our capture of the southern flying squirrel in the pine plantation is perhaps uncharacteristic for a species that prefers mature hardwood or mixed deciduous-coniferous forests (Linzey 1998); one was observed in GEWA by Painter and Eckerlin (1993) in a white oak tree. However, pine plantations in GEWA may provide suitable nest sites in tree cavities (Dolan and Carter 1977) and opportunities for movement (gliding) among the regularly spaced trees.

The river otter represents a new and important species record for GEWA. This mammal is restricted to permanent watersheds within its range and is often associated with beavers or beaver lodges in bodies of water with banked shores (Lariviere and Walton 1998). The bank of the Potomac River, where signs of otter were documented, the bordering Popes Creek where three were seen, and Digwood Swamp where a beaver lodge was found, would seem to provide important habitat for otters. Beavers typically are associated with flowing water or other habitats that permit dam construction (Linzey 1998); availability of food is an important factor in the suitability of a habitat for occupation (Jenkins and Busher 1979).

Exotic species
Dogs were observed on a few occasions in the park. We do not know if these animals are feral or merely individuals from adjacent residential neighborhoods (we suspect the latter).

House mice were not captured within the park but in 2003 were captured and more abundant (relative abundance = 1.3; T. L. Dolbeare, in prep.) than any other small mammal in an agricultural field just outside the park boundary and near pine plantation 1. Thus, it is likely that this species occurs in the park. Painter and Eckerlin (1993) previously detected this mammal within the park around barns and outbuildings where domestic livestock and their food were housed. The house mouse is introduced from Eurasia and commensal with humans, but often forms feral populations. It is commonly the most abundant mammal in cultivated fields (Linzey 1998).

21

Habitat-specific species diversity

The managed fields of GEWA supported the greatest species diversity and richness of small mammals among the principal habitats sampled. These fields supported grassland specialists, least shrews, meadow voles, and eastern harvest mice, and the two habitat generalists, the northern short-tailed shrew and white-footed deermouse. The comparatively high Brillouin index for this habitat was attributable to both greater richness and evenness than other habitats. Grassy fields provide important resources, especially food, for a variety of small mammals. Meadow voles subsist chiefly on available grasses, sedges, and herbaceous plants (Reich 1981). Harvest mice eat seeds of grasses and other herbaceous plants, green vegetation, and crickets and grasshoppers (Stalling 1997). Northern short-tailed shrews are often associated with meadow voles, and earthworms and millipedes make up most of their diet. Lepidopteran larvae (caterpillars), earthworms, spiders, crickets and grasshoppers, and beetles are important foods of least shrews (Whitaker and Mumford 1972). White-footed deer mice, although chiefly woodland creatures, visit fields to forage for insects and seeds and also use grasses to line their nests (Lackey et al. 1985).

The logged habitat provided the least diversity of small mammals despite the high sampling effort. Approximately 97% of individuals captured in this habitat type were white-footed deer mice. As indicated earlier, this species does especially well in such habitats. Our failure to capture shrews in logged areas may be attributable to two factors, lack of soil moisture due to the reduction in canopy and/or failure to use pitfall traps in this habitat.

Sampling Efficiency

Sherman traps are the industry standard for live capture of rodents and shrews of body mass ≥ 10 g (Mitchell et al. 1993) and were used with success to capture a number of species in a variety of habitats. However, for smaller species pitfall traps are more efficient (Szaro et al. 1988; Kirkland and Sheppard 1994). Our comparative success with pitfall traps demonstrates that these traps also can be effective in capturing northern short-tailed shrews and small rodents ≥ 10 g in size. However, we used these traps on a very limited basis specifically to target small shrews that cannot be captured by any other means. The placement of pitfall traps is labor-intensive, and these traps must be used as kill traps because small shrews are difficult to identify to species and sex without close examination of the dentition and internal reproductive anatomy.

Tomahawk traps baited with canned cat food were efficient at sampling medium-size mammals (especially mesocarnivores) that are secretive or elusive. Remote cameras were labor-intensive and not very productive but were useful in detecting and confirming the identification of individuals that left sign in frequently traveled terrain. Occasionally, they rendered the unexpected, such as the image of the white-footed deermouse in the grasp of the Barred Owl. Direct observation, especially while conducting trap sampling, is efficient for detecting sign and medium to large, nonsecretive species.

Conclusions and Management Recommendations

Although no General Management Plan currently exists for GEWA, objectives have been established by the Resources Management Plan that provide for the preservation, restoration, maintenance, and protection of the cultural and natural resources of the park. Our inventory of the mammals of GEWA addresses and provides for the future attainment of these objectives. Most important, it documents the presence of particular species of mammals, notes their habitat associations, describes sampling protocol and provides information that can be used to monitor mammal populations, and provides recommendations for their conservation and management.

The park supports a predictable assemblage of mammals, based on the types of habitat present. Both habitat generalist and specialist species are widely distributed geographically in the park, usually in reasonable abundance where they are found. Two of the most common mammals in eastern North America, the northern short-tailed shrew and white-footed deermouse, occur in most of the principal habitats (the latter in all); the white-footed deermouse is especially abundant, as it is in most habitats where it occurs. Similarly, other common species, such as meadow voles, eastern cottontail rabbits, gray squirrels, woodchucks, Virginia opossums, raccoons, and white-tailed deer, were trapped or observed frequently in their preferred habitats.

Especially noteworthy was the presence and relative abundance of two grassland species that either typically do not occur as dense populations or are relatively difficult to capture, or both. A number of least shrews were captured in one of the managed fields. These individuals were caught solely in Sherman traps. The use of pitfall traps in this habitat likely would have yielded an even greater number of individuals. These results suggest a relatively dense population of least shrews in the park. Also, the eastern harvest mouse was captured in several locations. Although this species does not appear to be abundant in the park, it is notable that current grassland management practices support this species.

Additional Inventories

Additional inventory and monitoring work should be conducted to determine the status of a number of the species we either detected in low numbers (e.g., the southeastern shrew, marsh rice rat, southern flying squirrel, long-tailed weasel) or could not confirm but that have been recorded previously (woodland vole, muskrat, house mouse, brown rat, and mink). Wetlands should be sampled more intensively with the use of more traps providing greater coverage over additional sampling periods. Based on the findings of Painter and Eckerlin (1993), it is likely that the marsh rice rat is distributed more widely within this habitat type than we found. We captured only two individuals of this species, which signals an inadequate sampling effort for wetland habitat. Selective attention to wetland habitat might result in documentation of the star-nosed mole (Condylura cristata). Additional locations in fields should be sampled to determine if least shrews are more widespread than we discovered. The third dimension of forests could be sampled so that a more accurate accounting of arboreal (e.g., the southern flying squirrel) and semiarboreal (e.g., the white-footed deermouse, Virginia opossum) species could be made. Sherman traps can be mounted in trees (Barry et al. 1984) using aluminum nails so that safety in future logging operations is not jeopardized. Pitfall trap arrays should be used more extensively for sampling to establish the presence and status of small shrew species. Pitfall traps must be used responsibly and with adequate supervision only after archeological compliance or oversight has been completed so that archeological remains are not disturbed and large numbers of individuals of any single species are not sacrificed. The range of the pygmy shrew includes all of Virginia (Linzey 1998), and it may be a resident of the park that was not revealed by our limited sampling effort with pitfall traps.

Habitat Management

Inventorying and monitoring activities will continue to provide important information on how habitats should be managed for the conservation of the park's natural resources. Wetlands are important to a number of mammals found in GEWA and should receive special consideration for conservation efforts. It may be desirable to regulate visitor use of areas where sensitive wetland species (e.g., the river otter) are found. Logged areas, and to a lesser extent pine plantations, did not support small mammal diversity. However, fields exhibited considerably more diversity and should be maintained and managed carefully to retain healthy populations of small mammals, which in turn sustain larger species. Properly scheduled mowing and prescribed burns, as per The Fire Management Plan (www.nps.gov/gewa/gewafiremp/gewawildfiremp2.htm), can be used to interrupt succession and maintain a diversity of herbaceous vegetation suitable to the resource requirements of a variety of mammal species.

Species Management

Management for the control of particular mammal species in GEWA might be warranted. Woodchucks are proliferating in the historic core of the park (R. Morawe, pers. Comm.). Individuals are plentiful in fields and burrow along fencelines, at the bases of trees, and beneath buildings. The use of fumigants or live trapping and relocation might be justifiable procedures to control the woodchuck population. Live trapping and relocation also might be useful in the elimination of problematic individuals such as foxes and weasels that prey on GEWA farm fowl (R. Morawe, pers. comm.).

The NPS might consider purchasing the agricultural field adjacent to pine plantation 1 so that it can be managed for native vegetation and mammal species. This field either supports or acts as a sink for a population of the nonnative house mouse, at least seasonally, based on captures of 10 individuals of this species at this location in the fall of 2003 (T. L. Dolbeare, in prep.). This species was more abundant than any other small mammal in this field, which is often the case in cultivated fields (Linzey 1998).

Based on total captures in multiple habitats, several occasions of multiple captures on the same day (including a remote photograph that shows two individuals), the extent of Sherman trap disturbances, and seasonal captures of distinct individuals (based on size), it is apparent that the raccoon is abundant in the park and is of special concern for several reasons. In numbers it can be a significant predator on bird and reptile eggs and nestlings. It is also the primary terrestrial reservoir of rabies in the Southeast, and raccoon rabies is easily spread to feral cats. Most cases of human exposure to rabies result from contact with cats (Gehrt 2003). Although measures to reduce the number of raccoons in GEWA may not be justified or practical, management practices that would reduce the consequences of human activities that sustain raccoon populations (e.g., frequent monitoring of picnic areas and trash disposal) can be intensified.

Based on frequent sightings (including a number of records obtained by remote photography) and abundant sign, the white-tailed deer would appear to be abundant in GEWA. When overabundant, deer potentially pose several problems. These can include an alteration of the stable state of a northern temperate forest (Stromayer and Warren 1997), which can affect understory cover important to mammals and birds. Also, deer serve as hosts to an extraordinary diversity of ectoparasites, including adult, breeding *Ixodes scapularis*, the black-legged tick that is the vector of the etiologic agent for Lyme disease, the spirochete, *Borrelia burgdorferi* (Miller et al. 2003). Monitoring the deer population (e.g., with pellet-group counts) and understory browse in the park is recommended. If such monitoring suggests that deer may be altering the habitat to the detriment of other fauna, management practices to control the deer population may be worthy of consideration, especially considering the abundance of the white-footed deermouse, a highly competent host for black-legged tick larvae and nymphs (Ostfeld 1997).

Populations of GEWA mammals we documented should be monitored, and efforts to confirm the presence or absence of those species expected to be residents should be continued. In addition to the impacts of larger species on systems, such as those described earlier, the roles of small mammals as critical components of biological communities has been recognized for some time (e.g., Chew 1978). Small mammals consume, transport, and deposit spores and mycelia of mycorrhizal fungi (Fogel and Trappe 1978; Maser et al. 1988) and seeds of many plant species, mix soil and decompose organic matter and litter, regulate invertebrate (e.g., insect) populations, and serve as prey for numerous terrestrial and avian predators (Sekgororoane and Dilworth 1995; Carey and Harrington 2001). Management decisions that can affect proper stewardship of natural systems necessarily rely on periodic assessments of species diversity and abundances from inventory and monitoring activities.

Literature Cited

ASM. 1998. Guidelines for the capture, handling, and care of mammals as approved by the American Society of Mammalogists. Journal of Mammalogy 79:1416-1431.

Barry, R. E., K. A. Boyce, and A. C. Sucke. 1999. Local distribution, habitat, and home range of the Appalachian cottontail (*Sylvilagus obscurus*) at Dolly Sods. Final report submitted to the Nongame Wildlife and Natural Heritage Program, West Virginia Division of Natural Resources.

Barry, R. E., Jr., M. A. Botje, and L. B. Grantham. 1984. Vertical stratification of *Peromyscus leucopus* and *P. maniculatus* in southwestern Virginia. Journal of Mammalogy 65:145-148.

Barry, R. E., Jr., and E. N. Francq. 1980. Orientation to landmarks within the preferred habitat by *Peromyscus leucopus*. Journal of Mammalogy 61:292-303.

Boyce, K. A. 2001. Distribution, seasonal home range, movements and habitat of the Appalachian cottontail, *Sylvilagus obscurus*, at Dolly Sods, West Virginia. M. S. thesis, Frostburg State University, Frostburg, Maryland.

Buckner, C. A., and D. J. Shure. 1985. The response of *Peromyscus* to forest opening size in the southern Appalachian mountains. Journal of Mammalogy 66:299-307.

Caldwell, R. S., and H. Bryan. 1982. Notes on distribution and habitats of *Sorex* and *Microsorex* (Insectivora: Soricidae) in Kentucky. Brimleyana 8:91-100.

Carey, A. B., and C. A. Harrington. 2001. Small mammals in young forests: implication for management for sustainability. Forest Ecology and Management 154:289-309.

Chapman, J. A., J. G. Hockman, and Ojeda C., M. M. 1980. Sylvilagus floridanus. Mammalian Species 136:1-8.

Chapman, J. A., and J. A. Litvaitis. 2003. Eastern cottontail: *Sylvilagus floridanus* and allies. Pp. 101-125 in Wild mammals of North America: biology, management, and conservation. 2nd ed. (G. A. Feldhamer, B. C. Thompson, and J. A. Chapman, eds.). John Hopkins University Press, Baltimore.

Chew, R. M. 1978. The impact of small mammals on ecosystem structure and function. Pp. 167-180 in Populations of small mammals under natural conditions (R. T. Hartman, ed.). Special Publication Series Vol. 5, Pymatuning Laboratory of Ecology, University of Pittsburgh.

Cypher, B. L. 2003. Foxes: *Vulpes* species, *Urocyon* species, and *Alopex lagopus*. Pp. 511-546 in Wild mammals of North America: biology, management, and conservation. 2nd ed. (G. A. Feldhamer, B. C. Thompson, and J. A. Chapman, eds.). John Hopkins University Press, Baltimore.

Dolan, P.G., and D. C. Carter. 1977. Glaucomys volans. Mammalian Species 78:1-6.

Dolbeare, T. L. In prep. Small mammal diversity and demography of the white-footed mouse, *Peromyscus leucopus*, in George Washington Birthplace National Monument in Virginia. M.S. thesis, Frostburg State University, Frostburg, Maryland.

Edwards, J., M. Ford, and D. Guynn. 2003. Fox and gray squirrels: *Sciurus niger* and *S. carolinensis*. Pp. 248-267 in Wild mammals of North America: biology, management, and conservation. 2nd ed. (G. A. Feldhamer, B. C. Thompson, and J. A. Chapman, eds.). John Hopkins University Press, Baltimore.

Fogel, R., and J. M. Trappe. 1978. Fungus consumption (mycophagy) by small animals. Northwest Science 52:1:31.

French, T. W. 1980. Sorex longirostris. Mammalian Species 143:1-3.

Gage, K. L., R. S. Ostfeld, and J. G. Olson. 1995. Nonviral vector-borne zoonoses associated with mammals in the United States. Journal of Mammalogy 76:695-715.

Gardner, A. L., and M. E. Sunquist. 2003. Opossum: *Didelphis virginiana*. Pp. 3-29 in Wild mammals of North America: biology, management, and conservation. 2nd ed. (G. A. Feldhamer, B. C. Thompson, and J. A. Chapman, eds.). John Hopkins University Press, Baltimore.

Gehrt, S. D. 2003. Raccoon: *Procyon lotor* and allies. Pp. 611-634 in Wild mammals of North America: biology, management, and conservation. 2nd ed. (G. A. Feldhamer, B. C. Thompson, and J. A. Chapman, eds.). John Hopkins University Press, Baltimore.

George, S. D., J. R. Choate, and H. H. Genoways. 1986. Blarina brevicauda. Mammalian Species 261:1-9.

Jenkins, S. H., and P. E. Busher. 1979. Castor canadensis. Mammalian Species 120:1-8.

Jones, C., W. J. McShea, M. J. Conroy, and T. H. Kunz. 1996. Capturing mammals. Pp. 115-122 in Measuring and monitoring biological diversity: standard methods for mammals (D. E. Wilson, F. R. Cole, J. D. Nichols, R. Rudran, and M. S. Foster, eds.). Smithsonian Institution Press, Washington, District of Columbia.

Kirkland, G. L., Jr. 1990. Patterns of initial small mammals after clearcutting of temperate North American forests. Oikos 59:313-320.

Kirkland, G. L., Jr., and P. K. Sheppard. 1994. Proposed standard protocol for sampling of small mammal communities. Pp. 277-283 in Advances in the biology of shrews (J. F. Merritt, G. L. Kirkland, Jr., and R. K. Rose, eds.). Special Publication of the Carnegie Museum of Natural History 18, Pittsburgh, Pennsylvania.

Koprowski, J. L. 1994. Sciurus carolinensis. Mammalian Species 480:1-9.

Krebs, C. J. 1999. Ecological methodology. 2nd ed. Addison Wesley Longman,Inc., Menlo Park, California, 620 pp.

Krebs, C. J. 2003. Programs for ecological methodology. 2nd ed.© Exeter Software, East Setauket, New York.

Kunz, T. H., R. Rudran, and G. Gurri-Glass. 1996. Appendix 2: Human health concerns. Pp. 255-264 in Measuring and monitoring biological diversity: standard methods for mammals (D. E. Wilson, F. R. Cole, J. D. Nichols, R. Rudran, and M. S. Foster, eds.). Smithsonian Institution Press, Washington, District of Columbia.

Kwiecinski, G. G. 1998. Marmota monax. Mammalian Species 591:1-8.

Lackey, J. A., D. G. Huckaby, and B. G. Ormiston. 1985. Peromyscus leucopus. Mammalian Species 247:1-10.

Lariviere, S., and L. R. Walton. 1998. Lontra canadensis. Mammalian Species 587:1-8.

Linzey, D. W. 1998. The mammals of Virginia. The McDonald & Woodward Publishing Co., Blacksburg, Virginia.

Lotze, J.-H., and S. Anderson. 1979. Procyon lotor. Mammalian Species 119:1-8.

Mammone, K. A. 1997. Small mammal communities of structurally diverse clearcuts and adjacent woodlands in western Maryland. M. S. thesis, Frostburg State University, Frostburg, Maryland.

Maser, C., Z. Maser, and R. Molina. 1988. Small-mammal mycophagy in rangelands of central and southeastern Oregon. Journal of Range Management 41:309-312.

McDiarmid, R. W., and D. E. Wilson. 1996. Data standards. Pp. 56-60 in Measuring and monitoring biological diversity: standard methods for mammals (D. E. Wilson, F. R. Cole, J. D. Nichols, R. Rudran, and M. S. Foster, eds.). Smithsonian Institution Press, Washington, District of Columbia.

McManus, J. J. 1974. Didelphis virginiana. Mammalian Species 40:1-6.

Merritt, J. F. 1987. Guide to the mammals of Pennsylvania. University of Pittsburgh Press for The Carnegie Museum of Natural History, Pittsburgh, Pennsylvania.

Miller, K. V., L. I. Muller, and S. Demarais. 2003. White-tailed deer: *Odocoileus virginianus*. Pp. 906-930 in Wild mammals of North America: biology, management, and conservation. 2nd ed. (G. A. Feldhamer, B. C. Thompson, and J. A. Chapman, eds.). John Hopkins University Press, Baltimore.

Mills, J. N., T. L. Yates, J. E. Childs, R. R. Parmenter, T. G. Ksiazek, P. E. Rollin, and C. J. Peters. 1995. Guidelines for working with rodents potentially infected with hantavirus. Journal of Mammalogy 76:716-722.

Mitchell, J.C., S.Y. Erdle and J.F. Pagels. 1993. Evaluation of capture techniques for amphibian, reptile, and small mammal communities in saturated forested wetlands. Wetlands 13:130-136.

NPS. 1998. Natural resource inventory & monitoring in national parks. NPS Inventory and Monitoring Informational Brochure. http://www.nature.nps.gov/im/imbroch.htm.

NPS. 2000. Guidance for the design of sampling schemes for inventory and monitoring of biological resources in national parks. National Park Service Inventory and Monitoring Program.

NPS. 2004. Strategic plan for George Washington Birthplace National Monument: fiscal year 2005-2008. www.nps.gov/applications/parks/gewa/ppdocuments/GEWA%20FY2005-FY2008.pdf.

NPS. 2005. Labeling natural history specimens. Conserve O Gram 11/6:1-4. www.cr.nps.gov/museum/publications/conserveogram/constoc.html

NPSpecies Proper: NPSpecies - The National Park Service Biodiversity Database. Secure online version. https://science1.nature.nps.gov/npspecies/web/main/start (accessed April 2010).

Ostfeld, R. S. 1997. The ecology of Lyme-disease risk. American Scientist 85:338-346.

Painter, H. F., and R. P. Eckerlin. 1993. The mammalian fauna and ectoparasites of George Washington Birthplace National Monument, Westmoreland County, Virginia. Banisteria 2:10-13.

Reich, L. M. 1981. Microtus pennsylvanicus. Mammalian Species 159:1-8.

Rosatte, R., and S. Lariviere. 2003. Skunks: genera *Mephitis, Spilogale,* and *Conepatus*. Pp. 692-707 in Wild mammals of North America: biology, management, and conservation. 2nd ed. (G. A. Feldhamer, B. C. Thompson, and J. A. Chapman, eds.). John Hopkins University Press, Baltimore.

Rudran, R. 1996. General marking techniques. Pp. 299-304 in Measuring and monitoring biological diversity: standard methods for mammals (D. E. Wilson, F. R. Cole, J. D. Nichols, R. Rudran, and M. S. Foster, eds.). Smithsonian Institution Press, Washington, District of Columbia.

Rudran, R., and M. S. Foster. 1996. Conducting a survey to assess mammalian diversity. Pp. 71-79 in Measuring and monitoring biological diversity: standard methods for mammals (D. E. Wilson, F. R. Cole, J. D. Nichols, R. Rudran, and M. S. Foster, eds.). Smithsonian Institution Press, Washington, District of Columbia.

Rudran, R., and T. H. Kunz. 1996. Appendix 1: Ethics in research. Pp. 251-254 in Measuring and monitoring biological diversity: standard methods for mammals (D. E. Wilson, F. R. Cole, J. D. Nichols, R. Rudran, and M. S. Foster, eds.). Smithsonian Institution Press, Washington, District of Columbia.

Sekgororoane, G. B., and T. G. Dilworth. 1995. Relative abundance, richness, and diversity of small mammals at induced forest edges. Canadian Journal of Zoology 73:1432-1437.

Sheffield, S. R., and H. H. Thomas. 1997. Mustela frenata. Mammalian Species 570:1-9.

Stalling, D. T. 1997. Reithrodontomys humulis. Mammalian Species 565:1-6.

Stromayer, K. A. K., and R. J. Warren. 1997. Are overabundant deer herds in the eastern United States creating alternate stable states in forest plant communities? Wildlife Society Bulletin 25:227-234.

Szaro, R. D., L. H. Simons, and S. C. Belfit. 1988. Comparative effectiveness of pitfalls and live-traps in measuring small mammal community structure. Pp. 224-230 in Management of amphibians, reptiles, and small mammals in North America. U.S. Department of Agriculture. Flagstaff, Arizona.

Webster, W. D., J. F. Parnell, and W. C. Biggs, Jr. 1985. Mammals of the Carolinas, Virginia, and Maryland. University of North Carolina Press, Chapel Hill, North Carolina.

Whitaker, J. O., Jr. 1974. Cryptotis parva. Mammalian Species 43:1-8.

Whitaker, J. O., Jr., and R. E. Mumford. 1972. Food and ectoparasites of Indiana shrews. Journal of Mammalogy 53:329-335.

Wilson, D. E., and D. M. Reeder (eds.). 2005. Mammal species of the world: a taxonomic and geographic reference (Vols. 1 and 2). 3rd ed. Johns Hopkins University Press, Baltimore.

Wolfe, J. L. 1982. Oryzomys palustris. Mammalian Species 176:1-5.

Yates, T. L., and D. J. Schmidly. 1978. Scalopus aquaticus. Mammalian Species 105:1-4.

Appendix A. Trapping schedule, habitats, locations, and efforts for 2002 in George Washington Birthplace National Monument.

Dates[1]	Habitat/Site[2]	Location[3]	Sherman Trap Configuration[4]	Trap Nights		
				Sherman	Medium	Tomahawk
7/16 - 7/19	MF 1	0331580 4228558	Grid (0.49)	196		16
7/16 - 7/19	PP 1	0332182 4229351	Grid (0.49)	196		16
7/23 - 7/26	FLD 1	0331790 4229083	Grid (0.49)	196		16
7/23 - 7/26	WL 1	0332829 4229190	Tran (0.30)	120		16
7/23 - 7/26	MF 2	0331895 4228757	Grid (0.49)	196		16
7/30 - 8/2	FLD 2	0331684 4228214	Grid (0.49)	196		16
7/30 - 8/2	WL 2	0331794 4228128	Tran (0.09)	36		
9/21 - 9/22	DF	0331728 4228954	Grid (0.49)	98		
11/9 - 11/10	FLD 3	0330830 4229657	Tran (0.24)	48		

[1] Dates are nights traps were open.
[2] DF = deciduous forest, FLD = field, MF = mixed forest, PP = pine plantation, WL = wetland.
[3] UTM coordinates are for middle of grid or one end of transect; zone 18. See Figure 3 for map of locations.
[4] Numbers in parentheses for Sherman trap configuration are effective sampling area in ha for grids (Grid) and effective sampling length in km for transects (Tran).

33

Appendix B. Capture record for mammals caught in George Washington Birthplace National Monument from July through November 2002.

**Sherman live traps were used to capture small mammals and Tomahawk traps to capture *Procyon lotor*.

Habitat/ site[1]	Total Trap Nights		Scientific Name	Common Name	Total captures	No. Individuals	Relative Abundance[2]
	Sherman	Medium Tomohawk					
MF 1	196	16	*Peromyscus leucopus*	White-footed deermouse	6	17	3.1
			Blarina brevicauda	Northern short-tailed shrew	1	1	0.5
PP 1	196	16	*Peromyscus leucopus*	White-footed deermouse	5	5	2.6
			Procyon lotor	Raccoon	2	2	-
WL 1	120	8	*Peromyscus leucopus*	White-footed deermouse	6	14	5.0
MF 2	196	16	*Peromyscus leucopus*	White-footed deermouse	5	10	2.6
DF	98		*Peromyscus leucopus*	White-footed deermouse	1	1	1.0
FLD 3	48		*Microtus pennsylvanicus*	Meadow vole	2	2	4.2
Pasture*		1	*Didelphis virginiana*	Virginia opossum	2	2	-

[1] DF = deciduous forest, FLD = field, MF = mixed forest, PP = pine plantation, WL = wetland.
*Targeted trapping resulting in capture of female and juvenile in 1 trap night using a large Tomahawk trap (see text).
[2] Relative abundances (individuals/100 TNs) were determined only for small mammals captured in Sherman traps.

35

Appendix C. Trapping schedule, habitats, locations, trap configurations, and efforts for Sherman traps for 2003 at George Washington Birthplace National Monument.

Dates[1]	Habitat/Site[2]	Location[3]	Trap Configuration[4]	Trap Nights
3/7 – 3/9	MF	0331824 4228854	Grid (1.10)	3049
4/11 – 4/13				
4/25 - 4/27				
5/9 – 5/11				
5/20 – 5/22				
6/10 – 6/13				
7/1 – 7/4				
7/15 – 7/18				
8/13 – 8/16				
8/28 – 8/31				
9/11 – 9/13				
10/3 – 10/5[T]				
10/10 – 10/12				
10/24 – 10/26				
11/7 – 11/9				
11/21 – 11/23				
12/5 – 12/7				
3/14 – 3/16	PP 1	0332166 4229380	Grid (1.10)	3105
4/11 – 4/13				
4/25 - 4/27				
5/9 – 5/11				
5/20 – 5/22				
6/10 – 6/13				
7/1 – 7/4				
7/15 – 7/18				
7/30 – 8/2				
8/13 – 8/16				
8/28 – 8/31				
9/11 – 9/13				
10/3 – 10/5				
10/10 – 10/12				
10/24 – 10/26				
11/7 – 11/9				
11/21 – 11/23				
12/5 – 12/7				

Appendix C. Trapping schedule, habitats, locations, trap configurations, and efforts for Sherman traps for 2003 at George Washington Birthplace National Monument (continued).

Dates[1]	Habitat/Site[2]	Location[3]	Trap Configuration[4]	Trap Nights
3/25 – 3/28	PT FLD 1	0331181 4229668	Tran (0.45)	120
3/25 – 3/28	PT FLD 2	0331325 4229320	Tran (0.45)	120
3/25 – 3/28	DigSwamp	0331689 4229560	Tran (0.32)	84
5/28 - 5/30				
4/11 – 4/13	LOG 1	0331943 4229002	Grid (1.12)	2850
4/25 - 4/27				
5/9 – 5/11				
5/20 – 5/22				
6/10 – 6/13				
7/1 – 7/4				
7/15 – 7/18				
7/30 – 8/2				
8/13 – 8/16				
8/28 – 8/31				
9/11 – 9/13				
10/3 – 10/5				
10/10 – 10/12				
10/24 – 10/26				
11/7 – 11/9				
11/21 – 11/23				
12/5 – 12/7				
5/28 – 5/30	MF/LOG	0331939 4228936	Tran (0.30)	520
6/16 – 6/18				
7/22 – 7/25				
8/5 – 8/8				
8/25 – 8/27				
9/5 – 9/7				
10/17 – 10/19				
11/14 – 11/16				
6/16 – 6/18	FLD 1	0331780 4229096	Tran (0.14)	322
7/22 – 7/25				
8/5 – 8/8				
8/25 – 8/27				
9/5 – 9/7				
10/17 – 10/19				
11/14 – 11/16				

Appendix C. Trapping schedule, habitats, locations, trap configurations, and efforts for Sherman traps for 2003 at George Washington Birthplace National Monument (continued).

Dates[1]	Habitat/Site[2]	Location[3]	Trap Configuration[4]	Trap Nights
6/16 – 6/18	LOG 2	0332116 4228937	Grid (0.32)	322
7/22 – 7/25				
8/5 – 8/8				
8/25 – 8/27				
9/5 – 9/7				
10/17 – 10/19				
11/14 – 11/16				
7/2 – 7/4	Barn	0331978 4228227	Random	21
7/18 – 7/21	WL 3	0331904 4228240	Tran (0.08)	20
7/22 – 7/25	PP 2	0331552 4228870	Grid (1.10)	196
8/5 – 8/8	WL 4	0331811 4228521	Tran (0.45)	120
10/24 – 10/26	DF in PP 1	0332166 4229380	Tran (0.15)	30

[1] Dates are nights Sherman traps were open at the habitat/site.
[2] DF = deciduous forest (within PP 1), FLD = field, LOG = logged area, MF = mixed deciduous-coniferous forest, MF/LOG = mixed forest/logged area edge, PP = pine plantation, WL = wetland. PT = near the Potomac River, DigSwamp = Digwood Swamp
[3] UTM coordinates (zone 18) are for middle of grid or one end of transect
[4] Numbers in parentheses for Sherman trap configuration are effective sampling area in ha for grids (Grid) and effective sampling length in km for transects (Tran).

Appendix D. Trapping schedule, habitats, locations, and efforts for Tomahawk, pitfall, and mole harpoon traps for 2003 at GEWA.

| Dates[1] | Habitat/Site[2] | Location[3] | Trap Nights[4] | | |
			Tomahawk	Pitfall	Mole Traps
3/25 – 3/28	DigSwamp	0331689 4229560	16^s, 8^m		
3/25 – 3/28	PT Pond	0331121 4229799	8^s, 4^m		
4/25 – 4/27	MF	0331824 4228854	59^m	[18]	
5/9 – 5/11					
5/20 – 5/22					
6/10 – 6/13					
7/1 – 7/4					
7/30 – 8/2[P]					
10/3 – 10/5					
10/10 – 10/12					
10/24 – 10/26					
11/7 – 11/9					
11/21 – 11/23					
12/5 – 12/7					
4/25 – 4/27	PP 1	0332166 4229380	51^m		
5/9 – 5/11					
5/20 – 5/22					
6/10 – 6/13					
7/1 – 7/4					
10/3 – 10/5					
10/10 – 10/12					
10/24 – 10/26					
11/7 – 11/9					
11/21 – 11/23					
12/5 – 12/7					

Appendix D. Trapping schedule, habitats, locations, and efforts for Tomahawk, pitfall, and mole harpoon traps for 2003 at GEWA (continued).

Dates[1]	Habitat/Site[2]	Location[3]	Trap Nights[4]		
			Tomahawk	Pitfall	Mole Traps
4/25 – 4/27	LOG 1	0331943 4229002	59^m		
5/9 – 5/11					
5/20 – 5/22					
6/10 – 6/13					
7/1 – 7/4					
10/3 – 10/5					
10/10 – 10/12					
10/24 – 10/26					
11/7 – 11/9					
11/21 – 11/23					
12/5 – 12/7					
6/10 – 6/12	PP 2	0331552 4228870		[63]	
7/1 – 7/4					
8/5 – 8/8	WL 4	0331811 4228521	12^s		
8/5 – 8/15	MF 1	0331588 4228558		[66]	
10/16 – 10/19	MF/LOG	0331939 4228936	3^s, 10^m		
11/14 – 11/16					
10/17 – 10/19	LOG 2	0332116 4228937	9^s		
10/10 – 10/12	WL 3	0331904 4228240	9^s, 3^m		
10/24-10/26	Dorm Lawn	0331876 4228250			32
11/6 - 11/9					
11/13 – 11/16					

[1] Dates are nights traps were open at the habitat/site.
     [P] Pitfall traps only used during this period at this location.
[2] LOG = logged area, MF = mixed deciduous-coniferous forest, MF/LOG = mixed forest/logged area edge, Pond = pond edge, PP = pine plantation, WL = wetland, PT = near the Potomac River, DigSwamp = Digwood Swamp
[3] UTM coordinates (zone 18) are for middle of spatially associated Sherman trap grid or one end of Sherman trap transect.
[4] Tomahawk traps ^{s} = small, ^{m} = medium

Appendix E. Capture record for mammals caught in George Washington Birthplace National Monument from March to December 2003.

Habitat/site[1]	TNs				Species name	Common name	No. individuals[3]	Total captures	Relative Abundance[4]
	Sherman	Tomahawk[2]	Pitfall	Mole Harpoon					
MF 2	3049	59[m]	18		Didelphis virginiana	Virginia opossum	?	3	-
					Blarina brevicauda	Northern short-tailed shrew	4	4	0.1
					Peromyscus leucopus	White-footed deermouse	26	53	0.8
					Mephitis mephitis	Striped skunk	?	2	-
					Procyon lotor	Raccoon	?	4	-
PP 1	3105	51[m]			Didelphis virginiana	Virginia opossum	?	3	-
					Blarina brevicauda	Northern short-tailed shrew	1	1	0.03
					Peromyscus leucopus	White-footed deermouse	32	96	0.9
					Glaucomys volans	Southern flying squirrel	1	1	0.03
LOG 1	2850	59[m]			Didelphis virginiana	Virginia opossum	?	2	-
					Peromyscus leucopus	White-footed deermouse	53	187	1.9
					Reithrodontomys humulis	Eastern harvest mouse	1	1	0.04
					Mustela frenata	Long-tailed weasel	1	1	0.04
					Procyon lotor	Raccoon	?	9	-
PT Field 1	120				Peromyscus leucopus	White-footed deermouse	4	6	3.3
					Microtus pennsylvanicus	Meadow vole	1	1	0.8
PT Field 2	120				Reithrodontomys humulis	Eastern harvest mouse	1	4	0.8
					Microtus pennsylvanicus	Meadow vole	4	5	3.3
DigSwamp	84	16[s], 8[m]			Peromyscus leucopus	White-footed deermouse	4	4	4.4
					Procyon lotor	Raccoon	?	2	-
PT Pond		8[s], 4[m]			Sylvilagus floridanus	Eastern cottontail	1	1	-
					Procyon lotor	Raccoon	1	1	-
MF/LOG	520	3[s], 10[m]			Blarina brevicauda	Northern short-tailed shrew	1	1	0.2
					Peromyscus leucopus	White-footed deermouse	15	43	2.9
					Procyon lotor	Raccoon	?	3	-

Appendix E. Capture record for mammals caught in George Washington Birthplace National Monument from March to December 2003 (continued).

Habitat/site[1]	TNs				Species name	Common name	No. individuals[3]	Total captures	Relative Abundance[4]
	Sherman	Tomahawk[2]	Pitfall	Mole Harpoon					
FLD 1	322				Cryptotis parva*	North American least shrew	7	7	2.2
					Blarina brevicauda	Northern short-tailed mouse	2	3	0.6
					Reithrodontomys humulis	Eastern harvest mouse	1	1	0.3
					Microtus pennsylvanicus	Meadow vole	3	5	0.9
LOG 2	322	9[s]			Didelphis virginiana	Virginia opossum	1	1	-
					Peromyscus leucopus	White-footed deermouse	11	18	3.4
Barn	21				Reithrodontomys humulis	Eastern harvest mouse	2	2	9.5
WL 3	20	9[s], 3[m]			Peromyscus leucopus	White-footed deermouse	2	2	10
					Oryzomys palustris	Marsh oryzomys (rice rat)	2	2	10
PP 2	196		63		Sorex longirostris**	Southeastern shrew	1	1	-
					Blarina brevicauda**	Northern short-tailed shrew	3	3	-
					Peromyscus leucopus	White-footed deermouse	7	19	3.6
					Peromyscus leucopus**	White-footed deermouse	4	4	-
WL 4	120	12[s]			Didelphis virginiana	Virginia opossum	1	1	-
					Blarina brevicauda	Northern short-tailed shrew	1	1	0.8
					Peromyscus leucopus	White-footed deermouse	8	16	6.7
DF in PP 1	30				Peromyscus leucopus	White-footed deermouse	3	5	10
Dorm law				32	Scalopus aquaticus	Eastern mole	1	1	-

[1] DF = deciduous forest (within PP 1), FLD = field, LOG = logged area, MF = mixed deciduous-coniferous forest, MF/LOG = mixed forest/logged area edge, Pond = pond edge, PP = pine plantation, WL = wetland.

[2] s = small Tomahawk traps, m = medium Tomahawk traps

* Identifications based on 4 of these individuals collected and prepared as voucher specimens

** Pitfall trap

[3] ? indicates that individuals were not marked for recognition upon recapture.

[4] Relative abundance is individuals/100 Sherman trap nights. Relative abundances are not determined for captures in Tomahawk, pitfall, or mole harpoon traps.

44

Appendix F. Voucher specimens (bats excluded) from George Washington Birthplace National Monument collected by Painter and Eckerlin (1993) and housed in the mammal collection at Northern Virginia Community College (NVCC), Annandale, Virginia.

Species Name	Common name	Sex	Date Collected	NVCC Number
Blarina brevicauda	Northern short-tailed shrew	M	19-Oct-86	6107
Scalopus aquaticus	Eastern mole	F	24-Apr-88	6356
Microtus pennsylvanicus	Meadow vole	F	24-Apr-88	6357
Microtus pinetorum	Woodland vole	M	18-Apr-87	6859
Mus musculus	House mouse	F	16-Jan-87	6165
Oryzomys palustris	Marsh oryzomys (rice rat)	M	19-Oct-86	6156
Oryzomys palustris	Marsh oryzomys (rice rat)	M	16-Jan-87	6167
Peromyscus leucopus	White-footed deermouse	M	16-Jan-87	6166

NPS 332/102045, April 2010

www.ingramcontent.com/pod-product-compliance
Lightning Source LLC
Chambersburg PA
CBHW080907290526
45795CB00007BA/2437